JUST ONE COOKBOOK

ESSENTIAL JAPANESE RECIPES

RECIPES + PHOTOGRAPHY
NAMIKO CHEN

INTERESTED IN LEARNING MORE
ABOUT JAPANESE COOKING?
VISIT US:

WWW.JUSTONECOOKBOOK.COM

JUST ONE

COOKBOOK

EASY JAPANESE RECIPES

CONTENTS

INTRODUCTION

Introduction: Essential Japanese Cooking.....6

BASICS + PANTRY

Dashi......11
Miso Soup......13
Steamed Rice......15
Sushi Rice......17
Pantry.....18

APPETIZERS

Agedashi Tofu...25
Chawanmushi......27
Salad with Sesame Dressing......29
Salad with Wafu Dressing......31
Teba Shio......33

SIDE DISHES

Gyoza...37
Hiyayakko......39
Spinach Gomaae......41
Sunomono......43
Tamagoyaki......45

MAIN DISHES

Chicken Teriyaki......49
Crispy Baked Chicken Katsu......51
Hambagu......53
Miso Cod.....55
Saikoro Steak......57
Salted Salmon.....59
Tempura.....61

RICE + NOODLES

California Roll...65
Gyudon......67
Kitsune Udon......69
Omurice......71
Oyakodon......73
Soba Salad.....75
Spicy Tuna Roll.....77

DESSERTS

Dorayaki...81
Flan......83
Green Tea Ice Cream......85
Green Tea Steamed Cake......87
Japanese Cheesecake......89

INDEX

Recipe Index.....91

JUST ONE COOKBOOK

INTRODUCTION

I learned almost everything I know about cooking Japanese food from my mother. When I was young, every evening, she would call me into the kitchen to cut veggies and help prep ingredients for dinner. She would not actually let me do the cooking, but I soon began to develop my skills, prep after prep. Needless to say, prepping food wasn't my favorite thing to do growing up! At the time I didn't know this, but all the prep work my mother guided me through would not only come in handy later in my life; this knowledge she gave me would soon become essential to my life.

When I left Japan at age twenty to attend college in the United States, I longed for one of my mother's home cooked Japanese meals. I soon realized that the only way to enjoy home cooked Japanese food was to cook it myself! Thanks to the time I had spent with my mom in the kitchen, night after night, I was able to create and enjoy a piece of home through cooking.

My mom was the one who taught me the fundamentals of Japanese cooking, guiding me through the different cooking methods. When I actually started to cook, I knew how to prepare ingredients; the actual cooking part became easier as I spent years watching my mother work her magic. I am now using all the tips and tricks she taught me to prepare home cooked Japanese meals for my husband, my son, my daughter and my friends here in the United States.

Preparing Japanese recipes for my family and friends grew into sharing recipes on Just One Cookbook for two reasons. First, I wanted to create a place where all my recipes could live so I could

JUST ONE COOKBOOK

pass them on to my children. My own mom never kept her recipes – how I wish she did! The second reason I created Just One Cookbook was to share quick and simple recipes with my friends who wanted to make Japanese food at home, but didn't have much experience in the kitchen.

In this Essential Japanese Recipes cookbook, I collected the most popular Japanese recipes from Just One Cookbook over the past 3 years. I hope you'll enjoy these recipes as much as my family and readers do. I want to thank the readers who inspired and encouraged me to create this cookbook. You'll find that these recipes are easy to prepare and the ingredients are rather easy to find. I hope as you prepare each appetizer, dish or dessert you'll be pleasantly surprised by how delicious they taste.

Happy Cooking!

Nami

FOUNDER + AUTHOR, WWW.JUSTONECOOKBOOK.COM

BASICS + PANTRY

DASHI

● ● ●

YIELD: 3½ CUPS

PREP: 5 MIN

COOK: 35 MIN

Used in many Japanese recipes, this stock is made from kombu (dried kelp), bonito flakes (shaved skipjack tuna), sardine, or a combination of all or two of them which creates a unique umami flavor.

INGREDIENTS

0.7 oz (20 g) **kombu**

3 cups (30 g) loosely packed **katsuobushi** (dried bonito flakes) - omit for vegetarian/vegan Kombu Dashi

4 cups (1000 ml) **water** (or 8 cups - see Note)

Notes:

1. If you don't need strong dashi flavor, you can replace 4 cups of water with 8 cups.

2. If you are not using dashi right away, save it in a bottle and keep in the refrigerator for 3-7 days or in the freezer for 3 weeks.

STEPS

1. Gently clean the kombu with a damp cloth, without removing the white powdery "umami" substances. Make a couple of slits on the kombu.

2. Put the kombu and water in a saucepan and soak for 2-3 hours (at least 30 minutes).

3. Slowly bring to a boil over medium low heat. Just before boiling, turn off the heat and remove the kombu. If you don't remove the kombu, the dashi will become slimy and bitter.

4. **For vegetarian Kombu Dashi,** strain the dashi through a sieve lined with a paper towel set over a bowl.

5. **For regular Dashi,** let the dashi cool a bit. Add the katsuobushi and bring it to a boil again. Once the dashi is boiling, reduce the heat and simmer for 30 seconds. Turn off the heat and let the katsuobushi sink to the bottom, about 10 minutes.

6. Strain the dashi through a sieve lined with a paper towel set over a bowl. Gently twist and squeeze the paper towel to release the extra dashi into the bowl.

DAIRY FREE (DF)   SOY FREE (SF)

VEGAN (VG) GLUTEN FREE (GF)

MISO SOUP

• • •

 SERVES: 3 - 4

 PREP: 5 MIN

COOK: 5 MIN

Most Japanese meals are served with a bowl of miso soup and steamed rice.

The secret to delicious miso soup is good dashi. Experiment and try adding seasonal ingredients to miso soup!

INGREDIENTS

3 cups **dashi**

3 Tbsp. **miso***

6 oz **silken tofu** or **soft tofu**, drained, cut into ½" (1 cm) cubes

2 tsp. dried ready-to-use **wakame** (seaweed), rehydrated

1 **green onion/scallion**, finely sliced

Notes:

1. For vegetarian miso soup, use kombu dashi.

2. For quick dashi, put 1¼ tsp. dashi powder (or 1 dashi packet) in 3 cups water.

3. Each brand or kind of miso has different level of saltiness; therefore, add miso 1 Tbsp. at a time and taste the soup before you add more miso.

STEPS

1. In a medium saucepan, bring dashi to a boil and turn off the heat.

2. Put 1 Tbsp. of miso in a ladle and scoop some dashi from the saucepan. Blend it until it is thoroughly mixed and pour back to the saucepan. Continue this process until miso is all used. Usually for each cup of dashi, you will need about 1 Tbsp. of miso.

3. Add tofu to the soup and stir gently without breaking the tofu. Return to a slight simmer until heated through. Be careful not to boil the miso soup because miso will lose flavor.

4. Place the wakame and green onion in each bowl. Pour miso soup into the bowls.

GLUTEN FREE

DAIRY FREE

VEGETARIAN/VEGAN

*Use gluten-free miso to make this recipe gluten-free.

STEAMED RICE

• • •

SERVES: 2-3

PREP: 5 MIN

 COOK: 15 MIN

The Japanese consider rice as the main course and most important part of the meal.

Enjoy tasty steamed rice without using a rice cooker.

INGREDIENTS

1 cup premium Japanese **short grain rice**

1¼ cups (300 ml) **water**

Note:

1. A heavy-bottom pot with a tight-fitting lid is recommended.

STEPS

1. Put rice in a large bowl. Gently wash the rice in a circular motion and discard the water. Repeat this process about 4-5 times until the water becomes almost translucent. Let the rice soak in water for 30 minutes. Transfer the rice into a sieve and drain for 15 minutes.

2. Combine the rice and water in a heavy bottom pot and bring it to a boil over medium heat. Take a quick peek to see if water is boiling (otherwise do not open the lid).

3. Once water is boiling, turn the heat to low and cook covered for 12 to 13 minutes, or until the water is completely absorbed (take a quick peek!). If you see there is water left, close the lid and continue cooking for a little longer.

4. Remove the pot (with the lid on) from the heat source and let it steam for another 10 minutes. Fluff the rice with a rice paddle when it's done.

DAIRY FREE (DF)   SOY FREE (SF)

VEGAN (VG) GLUTEN FREE (GF)

SUSHI RICE

• • •

 YIELDS: 4½ CUPS

 PREP: 15 MIN

COOK: 20 MIN

The delicate vinegared rice with delicious sashimi on top, it tastes like a little bit of heaven.

Enjoy making sushi rice at home with these simple instructions.

INGREDIENTS

2 cups premium Japanese **short grain rice**
2½ cups (600 ml) **water**
2" (5 cm) **kombu**

Sushi Vinegar
⅓ cup **rice vinegar**
3 Tbsp. **sugar**
1½ tsp. **salt**

Notes:

1. If you're using a rice cooker, follow the manufacturer's instructions for cooking sushi rice.

2. There are convenient Sushi Seasonings available at Japanese/Asian grocery stores.

STEPS

1. Put rice in a large bowl. Gently wash the rice in a circular motion and discard the water. Repeat this process about 4-5 times until the water becomes almost translucent. Let the rice soak in water for 30 minutes. Transfer the rice into a sieve and drain for 15 minutes.

2. Combine the rice and water in a heavy-bottom pot. Place the kombu on top of the rice and cook the rice according to **Steamed Rice** recipe.

3. To make sushi vinegar, combine rice vinegar, sugar, and salt in a small saucepan and bring it to a boil over medium high heat until the sugar is completely dissolved. Set aside to let it cool.

4. When the rice is cooked, moisten a large bowl with water so the rice will not stick. Transfer the cooked rice into the bowl and spread out evenly so the rice will cool faster. While it's hot, pour the sushi vinegar over the rice.

5. With a rice paddle, slice the rice to separate the rice grains instead of mixing, and flip the rice in between slices.

6. Keep the rice covered with a damp kitchen cloth (or paper towel) until ready to serve.

DAIRY FREE SOY FREE SF

VEGAN VG GLUTEN FREE

PANTRY BASICS

• • •

ABURAAGE: Fried tofu pouches used in Inari Sushi, miso soup, and simmered dishes. *Inariage* is made from aburaage with sweet seasoning and is used for Kitsune Udon and Inari Sushi.

CRAB STICKS: Kanikama or imitation crab, commonly used in sushi rolls as well as salads.

DAIKON: Japanese radish. Daikon is known to be digestive for oily foods; therefore, grated daikon is commonly served together with dipping sauce for oily food, such as tempura.

DASHI: Seafood based stock usually made from kombu (kelp), katsuobushi (dried bonito flakes), iriko/niboshi (sardine) or a combination of all or two of them. Dashi made with only kombu is vegetarian dashi.

DRIED SHIITAKE MUSHROOMS: Rehydrate in water and use as you would regular shiitake mushrooms. Reserve the soaking liquid for stocks, soups, and broths.

DRIED WAKAME: A type of seaweed used in miso soup, salad, and sunomono. Needs to be rehydrated in water prior to use.

GINKGO NUTS: Considered as delicacy and often used in Chinese and Japanese cuisine or medicine as they are believed to have health benefits. Commonly used in Chawanmushi.

GREEN TEA POWDER (MATCHA): A fine ground, powdered, high quality green tea, different from regular green tea. Matcha comes only from shade-grown tea leaves and is used for Japanese tea ceremonies and Japanese sweets.

GYOZA WRAPPERS: Wheat flour based wrappers used for pot stickers, usually thinner and smaller than Chinese pot sticker wrappers.

JAPANESE RICE: Short grain rice, Japonica species. Varieties include Koshihikari, Hitomebore, and Akitakomachi.

JAPANESE MAYONNAISE: Compared to European or American mayonnaise, Japanese mayonnaise is slightly tangy, sweeter, and creamier in both color and texture. For substituting with non-Japanese mayo, add 2 Tbsp. rice vinegar and 1 Tbsp. sugar in 1 cup of American mayo and whisk until the sugar dissolves.

KAMABOKO: A type of cured surimi, a Japanese processed seafood product, made from white fish fillet pounded into a paste, mixed with a starch and molded into a variety of shapes.

KATSUOBUSHI: Dried bonito fillet which is shaved into flakes. The bonito fillet is boiled, dried, then smoked and finally cured with a mold. It is then shaved to use for making dashi, or as a garnish or condiment.

KOMBU/KONBU: Dried kelp used for making dashi.

KOREAN CHILI THREADS: Ito togarashi. Fine slivers of Korean dried red chili peppers used as garnish.

LA-YU: Japanese chili oil.

MENTSUYU: Japanese soup base used in soba and udon noodle dishes. It's made from sake, mirin, soy sauce, kombu, and katsuobushi.

MIRIN: Sweet cooking sake. It's a rice wine similar to sake, but with a lower alcohol content (14% instead of 20%). Mirin tenderizes meats, adds a mild sweetness, and helps mask the smell of fish and seafood. It has deep body and umami flavor.

MISO: A fermented paste of soybeans, barley or rice, and salt. *Red miso* (aka miso) is mostly made with rice and is reddish brown in color. *White miso* (shiro miso) is used mostly in Western Japan recipes where Saikyo miso is popular. It's sweet and used for marinating fish. *Awase miso* is a combination of red and white miso, typically used for soup.

MITSUBA: Japanese wild parsley. A popular herb used as a garnish.

NARUTOMAKI: A type of kamaboko. Each slice of narutomaki or naruto has a pink spiral pattern which resembles the Naruto Whirlpools between Awaji Island and Shikoku in Japan.

NORI: Dried seaweed pressed into thin sheets and commonly used as a seasoning or as a wrapper for sushi.

PANKO: Japanese-style bread crumbs traditionally used as a coating for deep-fried foods like tonkatsu and Japanese croquette. They are larger, crispier and lighter than regular bread crumbs and made of bread without crusts.

PICKED RED GINGER (BENI SHOGA): A type of Japanese pickle made from ginger cut into thin strips, colored red, and pickled in plum vinegar.

PONZU: A dipping sauce made from a mixture of soy sauce, and citrus juice squeezed from daidai, kabosu, sudashi, or yuzu.

POTATO STARCH: Thickening starch. Can be substituted with corn starch.

RICE VINEGAR: This vinegar is made from rice and it is sweeter, milder, and less acidic than western vinegars. It is an essential ingredient in sushi rice and sunomono. It is also known for its anti-bacterial properties and that's the reason it is often used in Japanese dishes that include raw fish, seafood, and meat.

SAKE: Pronounced as SAH-keh, not saki. Sake is made from rice and water through a brewing process like beer.

SESAME OIL: Oil derived from sesame seeds. Besides its use as a cooking oil, it is also used as a flavor enhancer.

SESAME SEEDS: White (shiro) or black (kuro) sesame seeds should be toasted in a frying pan before using to give off a nice aroma.

SHICHIMI TOGARASHI: Japanese seven spice is a mixture of red chili flakes, sansho (Sicuhan pepper), sesame seeds, nori, and shiso, dried mandarin or orange peel, hemp and poppy seeds.

SHISO: Perilla leaf. Member of mint family and has a slightly basil-like flavor.

SOBA: A type of thin noodle made from buckwheat flour. Soba noodles are served either chilled with a dipping sauce or in hot broth as a noodle soup. Noodle shops in Japan usually offer soba or udon for noodle options.

SOY SAUCE: Shoyu. *Koikuchi shoyu* is most widely used and may not be labeled so but it is regular soy sauce. *Usukuchi shoyu* is a saltier and light-color soy sauce which is used when you don't want to discolor food material or sauce. *Tamari Shoyu* is darker, thicker, richer and less salty than most soy sauce. It is made with no (or little) wheat and greater concentration of soybeans. It is a great substitution for soy sauce if you are gluten intolerant. Tamari is traditionally used to season sashimi, teriyaki-style grilled dishes, and longer cooking food such as soups, stews, and braised dishes.

SUSHI ZU: Sushi vinegar. Seasonings added to steamed rice to make sushi rice. It's made of rice vinegar, sugar, and salt. You can make from scratch or you can buy from Asian grocery stores.

SWEET RED BEAN PASTE: Dark red sweet bean paste made of Azuki beans. It is used in Japanese confectionary (wagashi).

TOFU: It is also called bean curd, made from soybeans, water, and curdling agent. There are many different varieties of tofu, including fresh tofu (silken/soft, medium/regular, or firm), fried tofu, and tofu skin.

TONKATSU SAUCE: A type of thick Worcestershire sauce mainly used as dipping sauce for tonkastu and other fried foods like Japanese croquette.

UDON: Wheat noodles, available in fresh or dried form. Usually sold frozen in Asian grocery stores.

WASABI: Fresh wasabi is rare because it grows only in the wild and in cool shaded mountain streams. Outside of Japan, it is rare to find real wasabi plants. A common substitute for wasabi is a mixture of horseradish, mustard, starch, and green food coloring.

APPETIZERS

AGEDASHI TOFU......25
CHAWANMUSHI......27
SALAD WITH SESAME DRESSING......29
SALAD WITH WAFU DRESSING......31
TEBA SHIO......33

AGEDASHI TOFU

• • •

 SERVES: 3

 PREP: 15 MIN

COOK: 15 MIN

Deep fried silken tofu with a crispy outer shell, served in a hot sweet dashi broth. My favorite toppings include grated daikon, katsuobushi, and finely chopped scallion.

INGREDIENTS

1 block (14 oz) **silken tofu** (soft tofu)

4 Tbsp. **potato starch** (or corn starch)

Vegetable oil for deep frying

Sauce

1 cup **dashi**

2 Tbsp. **soy sauce** (use tamari if gluten-free)

2 Tbsp. **mirin**

Toppings

1" (2.5 cm) **daikon radish**, grated

1 **green onion/scallion**, thinly sliced

Katsuobushi (dried bonito flakes) (optional, and skip if vegetarian)

Shichimi togarashi (Japanese seven spice) (optional)

STEPS

1. Drain the tofu by wrapping tofu with 3-4 layers of paper towels and place on a plate. Place a flat plate on top of the tofu to squeeze the liquid out for 15 minutes.

2. Put dashi, soy sauce, and mirin in a saucepan and bring to a boil. Turn off the heat and set aside.

3. Remove tofu from paper towels and cut tofu into 8 pieces.

4. Heat the oil to 350°F (175°C) in a deep fryer.

5. Coat the tofu with potato starch and deep fry until they turn light brown and crispy.

6. Remove the tofu and drain excess oil on a plate lined with paper towels.

7. To serve, place the tofu in a serving bowl and pour the sauce on the tofu. Garnish with grated daikon, green onion, katsuobushi, and shichimi togarashi.

GLUTEN FREE

DAIRY FREE

VEGETARIAN/VEGAN

CHAWANMUSHI

• • •

 SERVES: 2

 PREP: 20 MIN

COOK: 30 MIN

A comforting and silky smooth egg custard steamed in a cup. This custard consists of an egg mixture flavored with dashi. Experiment and try adding your favorite ingredients.

INGREDIENTS

2 **dried shiitake mushrooms**
3 Tbsp. **water**
½ cup **dashi**
½ – 1 **chicken thigh**, rinsed and pat dry
½ Tbsp. **sake**
1 large **egg**
6 thin round slices **carrot**
6 precooked **ginkgo nuts**
1 ounce (30 g) brown **shimeji mushrooms**
6 thin slices **kamaboko** (fish cake)
4 **mitsuba** (Japanese wild parsley) or 1 green onion/scallion

Seasonings
½ tsp. **mirin**
¼ tsp. **salt**
¼ tsp. **soy sauce** (use tamari if gluten-free)

Toppings (optional)
2 pieces of **uni** (sea urchin)
2 Tbsp. **ikura** (salmon roe)

STEPS

1. In a small bowl, put dried shiitake and 3 Tbsp. of water and let it soak for 15 minutes. When shiitake becomes soft, slice it thinly and keep the liquid.

2. Put the liquid from Step 1 into a measuring cup and fill with dashi until you have ½ cup of liquid.

3. Cut chicken into bite size pieces and marinate chicken in sake for 15 minutes.

4. Whisk the egg in a medium bowl. Add the seasonings and dashi mixture from Step 2 into the bowl and mix well. Then strain the mixture through a fine sieve into another bowl.

5. Place two empty chawanmushi cups in a medium pot. Pour water until it covers half way up the exterior of the cups. Remove the cups and start boiling water.

6. Divide all the ingredients into chawanmushi cups and gently pour the egg mixture into the cups. Cover with the lid or use aluminium foil if lid is not available.

7. Once water starts boiling, reduce the heat to low. Place the cups gently inside the hot water and cover the pot. Cook for 25-30 minutes on the lowest heat. If you do not add chicken, the cooking time should be around 15-20 minutes.

8. Insert a skewer in the center of the cup to check if the egg is done. Put uni and ikura on top.

GLUTEN FREE
DAIRY FREE

SALAD WITH
SESAME DRESSING

• • •

 SERVES: 3-4

 PREP: 10 MIN

 COOK: 5 MIN

This popular dressing has a rich flavor of roasted sesame seed with a nice balance of creaminess and tanginess. I hope you'll enjoy this dressing as much as my family does.

INGREDIENTS

Salad
¼ head **Iceberg lettuce,** torn

Toppings (optional)
1 **tomato,** cut into wedges
1 **boiled eggs,** quartered
1 tsp. dried ready-to-use **wakame,** rehydrated
1 Tbsp. **frozen corn kernel,** cooked

Dressing
3 Tbsp. **white sesame seeds**
2 Tbsp. **Japanese mayonnaise**
2 Tbsp. **rice vinegar**
1 ½ Tbsp. **soy sauce** (use tamari if gluten-free)
1 tsp. **sugar**
½ tsp. **mirin**
½ tsp. **sesame oil**

STEPS

1. For the dressing, put sesame seeds in a frying pan and toast them on low heat. When 2-3 sesame seeds start popping, remove from the heat.

2. Grind the toasted sesame seeds with a mortar and pestle until smooth.

3. Combine all the ingredients in a bowl and whisk everything together.

4. Drizzle on top of a simple salad of iceberg lettuce topped with tomatoes, boiled eggs, wakame, and corn.

GLUTEN FREE

DAIRY FREE

VEGETARIAN

SALAD WITH
WAFU DRESSING
• • •

 SERVES: 3 - 4

 PREP: 10 MIN

 COOK: 0 MIN

Wafu means Japanese-style and this simple and delicious soy sauce based salad dressing is simply irresistible. Sweet, sour, and mixed with a bit of onion, it goes well with any salad.

INGREDIENTS

Salad
¼ head **Iceberg lettuce**, torn

Toppings (optional)
2 **tomatoes**, cut into wedges
2 **boiled eggs**, quartered
2 tsp. dried ready-to-use **wakame**, rehydrated
½ **Japanese cucumber** (English cucumber/Persian cucumber), thinly sliced
2 **red radishes**, thinly sliced

Dressing
1 Tbsp. grated **onion** with juice
3 Tbsp. **vegetable oil**
3 Tbsp. **soy sauce** (use tamari if gluten-free)
3 Tbsp. **rice vinegar**
1 Tbsp. **sugar**
Freshly ground **black pepper**
½ Tbsp. roasted **white sesame seeds**

STEPS

1. For the dressing, combine all the ingredients in a bowl and whisk everything together.

2. Drizzle on top of a simple salad of iceberg lettuce topped with tomatoes, boiled egg, wakame, cucumber and red radish.

GLUTEN FREE
DAIRY FREE
VEGETARIAN

TEBA SHIO

• • •

SERVES: 3-4

PREP: 5 MIN

COOK: 25 MIN

Typically served in Japanese tapas or izakaya restaurants, this tasty wings recipe is quick and easy to prepare at home! Just four simple ingredients: chicken wings, sake, salt, and pepper.

INGREDIENTS

2 lbs. (16 pieces) **chicken wings** (mid joints), rinsed
1½ cups **sake**
Sea salt
Freshly ground **black pepper**
Shichimi togarashi (Japanese seven spice) (optional)
Lemon wedges (optional)

STEPS

1. Adjust an oven rack to the middle position. Line the bottom of a broiler pan with aluminum foil and place the broiler rack on top.

2. Soak the chicken wings in sake for 10-15 minutes. Pat dry each wing with a paper towel and place the wing, skin side up, on the broiler rack.

3. Sprinkle a generous amount of salt and pepper, and flip the wings to sprinkle the other side. Keep the skin side down.

4. Turn the broiler on high and place the broiler pan in the oven about 6" (15 cm) away from the heat element. Cook for 15 minutes and flip to cook the other side (skin side) for 10 minutes.

5. Serve with shichimi togarashi and lemon wedges on the side.

GLUTEN FREE

DAIRY FREE

SOY FREE

SIDE DISHES

GYOZA.......37
HIYAYAKKO.......39
SPINACH GOMAAE.......41
SUNOMONO.......43
TAMAGOYAKI.......45

GYOZA

• • •

 YIELDS: 40 PIECES

 PREP: 30 MIN

COOK: 30 MIN

If you ask my children what their top 5 Japanese dishes are, gyoza is definitely on that list. Japanese gyoza (dumplings) are pan-fried till crisp and then steamed. Dip in vinegar soy sauce to enjoy. Add La-Yu to the sauce if you prefer spicy food!

INGREDIENTS

1 package **gyoza wrappers**
1 ½ Tbsp. **oil** for frying each batch of gyoza
¼ cup **water** for frying each batch of gyoza
1 Tbsp. **sesame oil** for frying each batch of gyoza
Filling
10 ounce (290 g) **ground pork**
2-3 **cabbage leaves**, cooked in a microwave for 1 minute and finely chopped
1 **green onion/scallion**, finely chopped
1-2 **shiitake mushrooms**, finely chopped
1 clove **garlic**, minced
1 tsp. **grated ginger**
Seasonings
½ Tbsp. **sake**
½ Tbsp. **sesame oil**
1 tsp. **soy sauce**
¼ tsp. **salt**
Freshly ground **black pepper**
Dipping Sauce
1 Tbsp. **rice vinegar**
1 Tbsp. **soy sauce** (use tamari if gluten-free)
⅛ tsp. **La-Yu** (Japanese chili oil) (optional)

STEPS

1. Combine the filling ingredients and seasonings in a large bowl and knead the mixture with hands until the texture becomes sticky.

2. Wrap the filling with gyoza wrappers (See How To Wrap Gyoza).

3. Heat the oil in a large non-stick pan over medium high heat. When the pan is hot, place the gyoza in a single layer, flat side down.

4. When the bottom of the gyoza turns golden brown, add ¼ cup of water to the pan and immediately cover with a lid. Steam the gyoza for about 2 minutes or until most of the water evaporates.

5. Remove the lid to evaporate any remaining water. Add sesame oil and cook uncovered until the gyoza is nice and crisp on the bottom. Transfer to a plate.

6. For the dipping sauce, combine the sauce ingredients in a small plate and mix all together. Serve the gyoza with the dipping sauce.

Notes:

1. After you wrap gyoza, cook or freeze it right away; otherwise water from the ingredients will start to make the wrapper wet.

2. To save gyoza for later, put the gyoza on a baking sheet leaving some space between to keep them from sticking, and put it in freezer. Transfer frozen gyoza into a freezer bag and store in freezer up to a month.

3. When you use frozen gyoza, do not defrost. Cook while they are frozen.

DAIRY FREE (DF)

HIYAYAKKO

● ● ●

○ SERVES: 4-6

○ PREP: 5 MIN

○ COOK: 0 MIN

This traditional chilled tofu is a delightful dish to enjoy during hot weather. My favorite toppings includes shiso leaves, cucumber, wakame, and tomatoes. So simple, yet so exquisite!

INGREDIENTS

1 block (14 oz) **silken tofu** (soft tofu), chilled
4 Tbsp. **katsuobushi** (dried bonito flakes)
1 **green onion/scallion,** thinly sliced
2 tsp. grated **ginger**
2 Tbsp. **soy sauce** (use tamari if gluten-free) or **ponzu sauce** (Japanese citrus-based sauce)

STEPS

1. Cut chilled tofu into 4-6 pieces.

2. Put each piece of tofu on a serving plate and top with katsuobushi, green onion, and grated ginger. Pour soy sauce on top before serving.

GLUTEN FREE (GF)
DAIRY FREE (DF)

SPINACH GOMAAE

• • •

Spinach or green beans are often served in sesame dressing (goma-ae) in Japanese cuisine. The delicate texture of freshly ground sesame seeds pairs very well with flavorful vegetables.

SERVES: 4

PREP: 15 MIN

COOK: 5 MIN

INGREDIENTS

1 bunch (½ lb., 220 g) **spinach**, rinsed thoroughly
A pinch of **salt**

Sesame Sauce
3 Tbsp. roasted **white sesame seeds**
1½ Tbsp. **soy sauce** (use tamari if gluten-free)
1 Tbsp. **sugar**
½ tsp. **sake**
½ tsp. **mirin**

Note:
1. American spinach is very soft and we can eat it raw unlike Japanese spinach; therefore, cooking for 1 minute is more than enough.

STEPS

1. Bring lightly salted water to a boil in a large pot. Add the spinach to boiling water from the stem side and cook for 1 minute.

2. Drain and soak the spinach in cold water until cool. Collect the spinach and squeeze water out. Cut the spinach into 2" (5 cm) lengths.

3. For sesame sauce, put sesame seeds in a frying pan and toast them on low heat. When 2-3 sesame seeds start to pop from the pan, remove from the heat.

4. Grind the toasted sesame seeds with a mortar and pestle until smooth.

5. In a bowl, combine the ground sesame seeds with soy sauce, sugar, sake, and mirin and mix all together.

6. Toss spinach and sesame sauce together and serve at room temperature or chilled.

GLUTEN FREE

DAIRY FREE

VEGETARIAN/VEGAN

SUNOMONO

• • •

Sunomono (*cucumber salad*) is a light, refreshing vinegar salad with cucumber that is a great start to a meal. The sourness from the vinegar helps open your appetite.

 SERVES: 2

 PREP: 10 MIN

COOK: 5 MIN

INGREDIENTS

1 Tbsp. dried ready-to-use **wakame** (seaweed), rehydrated

1 **Japanese cucumber** (½ English cucumber), thinly sliced

1 tsp. **salt**

½ tsp. julienned **ginger** (optional)

Dressing
3 Tbsp. **rice vinegar**
2 Tbsp. **dashi** or **water**
1 Tbsp. **sugar**
1 Tbsp. **soy sauce** (use tamari if gluten-free)
½ Tbsp. **sesame oil**

STEPS

1. Peel and slice the cucumber into very thin slices. Sprinkle the cucumber slices with salt and massage them. Let stand for a few minutes and squeeze out excess water from cucumber. Transfer to a bowl and add wakame.

2. Combine the dressing ingredients in a small saucepan and cook over high heat until the sugar dissolves completely. Set aside to cool.

3. Before serving, pour the dressing over cucumber slices and wakame and mix well together.

4. Serve in individual dishes and garnish with ginger on top.

GLUTEN FREE

DAIRY FREE

VEGETARIAN/VEGAN

TAMAGOYAKI

• • •

 SERVES: 2

 PREP: 5 MIN

COOK: 5 MIN

Tamagoyaki (*Japanese rolled omelette*) can be enjoyed as a side dish by itself or served on top of sushi. The many layers of this slightly sweet egg omelette give it a unique texture.

INGREDIENTS

3 large **eggs**
Seasonings
4 Tbsp. **dashi**
1 Tbsp. **sugar**
1 tsp. **soy sauce** (use tamari if gluten-free)
1 tsp. **mirin**
1 pinch of **salt**
Served with
Grated **daikon radish**, squeeze water out
Soy sauce (use tamari if gluten-free)

What you will need
Tamagoyaki frying pan (or a round 8-9 inch non-stick pan)

Chopsticks
Note:
1. Control the temperature of the pan by lifting the frying pan rather than adjusting the stove heat. If the heat is too weak, the egg will stick to the frying pan so be careful.

STEPS

1. Combine eggs and seasonings in a bowl and whisk gently (do not over mix). Strain the egg mixture through a sieve into a measuring cup with a handle (so it's easier to pour later).

2. Heat the pan over medium high heat, dip a folded paper towel in oil and apply oil to the pan.

3. When the pan is hot, pour a thin layer of egg mixture in the pan, tilting to cover the bottom of the pan. After the bottom of the egg has set but still soft on top, start rolling into a log shape from one side to the other.

4. Move the rolled omelette to the side where you started to roll, and apply oil to the pan with a paper towel, even under the omelette.

5. Pour the egg mixture to cover the bottom of the pan again. Make sure to lift the omelette to spread the mixture underneath. When the new layer of egg has set and still soft on top, start rolling from one side to the other.

6. Repeat this process until the egg mixture is used up.

7. Remove from the pan and slice the omelette into ½" (1 cm) pieces. Serve with grated daikon and soy sauce.

GLUTEN FREE

DAIRY FREE

VEGETARIAN

MAIN DISHES

CHICKEN TERIYAKI......49
CRISPY CHICKEN KATSU......51
HAMBAGU......53
MISO COD......55
SAIKORO STEAK......57
SALTED SALMON......59
TEMPURA......61

CHICKEN TERIYAKI

• • •

SERVES: 2

PREP: 10 MIN

COOK: 20 MIN

Teriyaki is a Japanese cooking technique: *teri* means "luster" which is given by the sweet soy sauce marinade and *yaki* means "cooking/grilling".

INGREDIENTS

1 lb. (454 g) **boneless chicken thigh with skin**, rinsed and pat dry
1 Tbsp. **oil** for step 4
2 Tbsp. **sake**
1 tsp. **oil** for step 6

Teriyaki Sauce
2 Tbsp. **soy sauce** (use tamari if gluten-free)
2 Tbsp. **water**
1 Tbsp. **sake**
1 Tbsp. **mirin**
1 Tbsp. **sugar**
¼ **onion**, grated, including juice
1" (2.5 cm) **ginger**, grated, including juice

STEPS

1. Combine the teriyaki sauce ingredients in a medium bowl.

2. Cut each chicken thigh into 4 pieces. Prick the chicken with a fork so it absorbs more flavor.

3. Add the chicken into the bowl and marinate for at least 2-3 hours in the refrigerator.

4. Heat the oil in a non-stick pan over medium high heat and place the chicken pieces skin side down, reserving the sauce. Cook until chicken is nicely browned. Then flip the chicken and add sake. Quickly cover the pan and cook over medium heat for 8-10 minutes.

5. Remove the chicken to a plate and wipe off excess grease from the pan.

6. Heat the oil and put the chicken back in the pan, skin side down, and cook until the skin becomes crispy.

7. Flip the chicken and pour the reserved sauce and cook until the sauce is reduced. Use a spoon to pour the sauce on top of the chicken while cooking.

8. Transfer the chicken to a plate and drizzle the remaining sauce on top.

GLUTEN FREE

DAIRY FREE

49

CHICKEN KATSU

• • •

Crispy outside and moist inside, this chicken katsu recipe is one of our family's favorite recipes. Simply coat the chicken with toasted panko and bake.

SERVES: 4

PREP: 15 MIN

COOK: 25 MIN

INGREDIENTS

1 cup **panko**

1 Tbsp. **olive oil**

1 lb. (454 g) **boneless, skinless chicken breast,** rinsed and pat dry

Salt

Freshly ground **black pepper**

¼ cup **all-purpose flour**

1 large **egg**

1 Tbsp. **water**

Tonkastu sauce

STEPS

1. Adjust an oven rack to the middle position and preheat the oven to 400°F (200°C). Line a rimmed baking sheet with parchment paper.

2. Combine the panko and oil in a frying pan and toast over medium heat until golden brown. Transfer panko into a shallow dish and allow to cool.

3. Butterfly and cut the chicken breast in half. Pound the chicken to equal thickness if necessary. Sprinkle salt and pepper on both sides of the chicken.

4. In a shallow dish, add flour and in another shallow dish, whisk together the egg and water.

5. Dredge each chicken piece in the flour to coat completely, pat off the excess flour. Then dip into the egg mixture and finally coat with the toasted panko. Press on the panko flakes to make sure they adhere to the chicken.

6. Place the chicken pieces on the prepared baking sheet.

7. Bake until the chicken is no longer pink inside, about 25-30 minutes. Serve with tonkastsu sauce.

DAIRY FREE (DF)

51

HAMBAGU

• • •

 SERVES: 4

 PREP: 20 MIN

COOK: 25 MIN

This tender & moist Hamburger Steak is a popular dish in Japanese diners. Enjoy it with the homemade sauce and your favorite glass of wine.

INGREDIENTS

1 Tbsp. **oil** for sautéing onion

½ (6.8 oz, 192 g) large **onion**, finely minced

¼ tsp. **salt**

Freshly ground **black pepper**

¾ lb. (14 oz, 386 g) **ground beef and ground pork** (50% beef and 50% pork)

1 large **egg**

2 Tbsp. **milk**

⅓ cup **panko**

1 tsp. **salt**

Freshly ground **black pepper**

½ tsp. **nutmeg**

1 Tbsp. **oil** for cooking Hambagu

¼ cup **red wine**

Sauce

1 Tbsp. **butter**

3 Tbsp. **red wine**

3 Tbsp. **water**

3 Tbsp. **ketchup**

3 Tbsp. **tonkatsu sauce** (or Worcestershire sauce)

STEPS

1. Heat the oil in a large pan over medium high heat. Sauté the onion until translucent and season with salt and pepper. Transfer to a large bowl and let it cool.

2. Add the meat in the bowl and mix all together. Then add the egg, milk, panko, salt, black pepper, and nutmeg, and knead well with your hands until the mixture gets sticky.

3. Make 4 large meatballs from the mixture and toss each one from one hand to the other repeatedly about 5 times to release the air pockets inside. Make meatballs into an oval shape about ¾" (2 cm) in height. Cover with plastic wrap and keep in the fridge for at least 30 minutes before cooking so that the mixture combines together.

4. Heat the oil in a large non-stick pan over medium heat and place the patties gently in the pan. Indent the center of each patty ¼" (.5 cm) with 2 fingers. Cook the patties for about 5 minutes or until nicely browned.

5. Flip the patties and pour red wine. Lower the heat to medium low heat and cook covered for 5 minutes or until the meat is cooked through. Uncover and increase the heat to medium high to let the remaining wine evaporate. When the liquid is almost gone, transfer hambagu into individual plates. Do not wash the pan.

6. Add the sauce ingredients in the same pan and mix well. Lower the heat to medium low and simmer for a few minutes, skimming off the scum and fat. When the sauce thickens, pour it over the hambagu.

DAIRY FREE DF

MISO COD

• • •

 SERVES: 2

 PREP: 10 MIN

COOK: 25 MIN

Made famous by the chef Nobu Matsuhisa, this black cod marinated in sweet miso becomes silky and buttery when cooked. It simply melts in your mouth!

INGREDIENTS

2 black cod (Gindara) fillets (you can also use salmon, sea bass, etc.)
2 tsp. **salt**
2 Tbsp. **sake**
Chives for garnish (optional)

Miso Marinade
3 Tbsp. **saikyo miso** (or white miso)
1½ Tbsp. **mirin** (if you use white miso, use 2 Tbsp. mirin instead)
1½ Tbsp. **sake**

STEPS

1. Sprinkle salt over the fillets and set aside for 30 minutes. This will help get rid of the fishy smell and remove excess moisture from the fish.

2. Wet a paper towel with sake and gently pat the fillets dry. Do not wash the fish.

3. Mix the marinade ingredients in a bowl and put half of mixture on the bottom of an air-tight container (with lid). Place the fillets in the container and slather the fillets with the remaining mixture. Cover the lid and keep in the fridge to marinate for 2-3 days (at least overnight).

4. Preheat oven to 400°F (200°C). Remove the marinade off the fillets completely with your fingers. Do not leave excess miso on the fish otherwise it'll burn easily.

5. Place the fish skin side up on baking pan lined with parchment paper. Bake the fish until the edges are browned and the fish is opaque, about 20-25 minutes. Do not flip the fish while baking.

GLUTEN FREE

DAIRY FREE

SAIKORO STEAK

• • •

Bite sized juicy steaks served with grated daikon and refreshing citrus ponzu. It's hard to stop eating after just one.

 SERVES: 2 AS MAIN, 4 AS APPETIZER

 PREP: 10 MIN

 COOK: 10 MIN

INGREDIENTS

About ¾ lb. (14 oz, 400 g) **tenderloin steak**, at room temperature
Salt
Freshly ground **black pepper**
2" (5 cm) **daikon radish**
1½ Tbsp. **oil**
2 cloves **garlic**, finely sliced
2 Tbsp. **dry sherry** (white wine)
1 **green onion/scallion** for garnish, finely sliced
Korean chili threads for garnish (optional)
3 Tbsp. **ponzu sauce**

Note:

1. A stainless steel pan is recommended for this recipe as steaks are required to cook on high heat. Most non-stick pans are not designed for use at high heat.

STEPS

1. Trim off the fat and tendons from the steak and cut into 1 to 1½" (2.5 to 3.5 cm) cubes. Season the steak with salt and pepper.

2. Peel and grate the daikon. Drain the liquid from the grated daikon and set aside.

3. Heat the oil in a large stainless steel frying pan over medium heat. Fry the sliced garlic until slices are golden brown. Reduce the heat if necessary so garlic slices do not burn. Transfer the garlic slices to a paper towel to drain excess oil. Keep the garlic infused oil in the pan.

4. Heat the oil over high heat until it begins to smoke. Pat dry the meat with a paper towel and place in the pan in a single layer.

5. Cook the steak until browned, about 1 minute. Don't move the steak until the bottom browns and releases on its own. Flip the steak over to continue cooking the other side till nicely browned.

6. Pour the wine and shake the pan to evenly distribute the wine in the pan. Transfer to a plate if you like medium rare steak. For medium steak, continue cooking for 1 more minute.

7. To serve, place the garlic slices, grated daikon and chopped green onion on top of the steak. Garnish with Korean chili threads if available. Pour ponzu sauce over the grated daikon before serving.

DAIRY FREE (DF)

SALTED SALMON

• • •

SERVES: 4

PREP: 10 MIN

COOK: 25 MIN

This salted salmon dish is usually served with a traditional Japanese-style breakfast or a hearty bento box lunch. Use leftovers as filling for onigiri (rice ball).

INGREDIENTS

1.1 lb. (500 g) **salmon fillets with skin**
1 Tbsp. **sake**
5 tsp. (25 g) **sea salt** (5% of salmon weight)
Lemon wedges (optional)

STEPS

1. Rinse the salmon under cold water and pat dry with a paper towel. Slice the salmon diagonally if it's not pre-sliced.

2. Pour and spread the sake on the salmon. After 10 minutes, pat dry the salmon with a paper towel.

3. Apply sea salt on the skin first, and then sprinkle the remaining salt on both sides of the fillets. Use more salt on the skin.

4. Line the bottom of an air-tight container (with lid) with a paper towel. This will absorb excess moisture from the fish. Place the fillets in the container in a single layer and lay a sheet of paper towel on top of the fillets. Then put the 2nd layer of the fillets on top of paper towel and lay another sheet of paper towel on top. Cover with lid and keep in the refrigerator for at least 2 days.

5. After 2 days, gently pat dry the fillets with a paper towel to get rid of any excess moisture.

6. Place the fillets on parchment-lined baking sheet. Make sure the skin side is up so the skin will become nice and crispy after baking. Bake at 400°F (200°C) for 20-25 minutes, or until the flesh is firm. Serve with lemon.

7. If you don't plan on cooking the salmon right away, after drying the fillets with a paper towel, wrap the individual pieces with plastic wrap and place them in a freezer bag to freeze. You can store the salmon in the freezer for up to 1 month. Remember to defrost before cooking.

DAIRY FREE (DF)
SOY FREE (SF)
GLUTEN FREE (GF)

59

SHRIMP TEMPURA

• • •

My children simply love crispy prawns covered in the tempura batter. Enjoy with tempura sauce or use in a sushi roll.

INGREDIENTS

Tempura Ingredients
10 large **shrimps**
Oil for deep frying (Vegetable oil : Sesame oil = 10 : 1)

Tempura Batter (egg water mixture: flour = 1 : 1)
1 cup (240 ml) **egg water mixture** (1 cold large egg (40 ml) + 200 ml iced water)
1 cup (240 ml) cold **all-purpose flour**

Tempura Sauce
¾ cup (200 ml) **dashi**
3 Tbsp. **soy sauce**
2 Tbsp. **mirin**
2 tsp. **sugar**
2" (5 cm) **daikon radish**, grated

Notes
1. Make batter right before deep frying to avoid activation of wheat gluten.
2. When you put too many shrimps, the oil temperature will drop quickly. Make sure to keep the right temperature for frying at all times.
3. For vegetarian tempura, you can use vegetables such as sweet potato, Kabocha squash, lotus root, King Oyster mushrooms, etc. Instead of regular dashi, vegetarians can use kombu dashi.

STEPS

1. To make tempura sauce, combine dashi, soy sauce, mirin, and sugar in a small saucepan and bring to a boil. Then remove from the heat and set aside. Grate the daikon and squeeze the liquid out. Place the grated daikon on a corner of a serving plate.

2. Peel the shell from shrimp and devein. Flip the shrimp over, belly side up, and holding onto the tail, make 4-5 very shallow perpendicular cuts along the length of the belly (do not slice all the way through the shrimp). Using your fingertips, gently press up the shrimp to straighten and lengthen it.

3. In a deep fryer, heat 1½" (3 cm) of the oil to 356°F (180°C).

4. To make the batter, combine the egg and iced water in a small bowl and whisk vigorously. Put flour in a medium bowl and slowly add the egg water mixture into the bowl. Mix the batter but do not over mix, it's okay to leave some lumps in batter. Keep the batter cold at all times.

5. Coat the shrimp with batter and fry until golden brown. Do not over crowd the fryer with shrimps; leave at least half of oil surface empty.

6. Transfer cooked shrimp tempura to a wired rack or a plate lined with a paper towel to drain excess oil. Between batches, remove the crumbs which will burn and turn the oil darker if left in fryer.

7. Serve with warm tempura sauce and grated daikon.

DAIRY FREE (DF)

RICE & NOODLES

CALIFORNIA ROLL......65

GYUDON......67

KITSUNE UDON......69

OMURICE......71

OYAKODON......73

SOBA SALAD......75

SPICY TUNA ROLL......77

CALIFORNIA ROLL

• • •

 YIELDS: 8 ROLLS

 PREP: 60 MIN

COOK: 0 MIN

An inside out sushi roll with savory crab & creamy avocado. Use different toppings like sesame seeds, ikura, or tobiko!

INGREDIENTS

8 cups **prepared sushi rice**
9 oz (255 g) **cooked crab meat**
6 Tbsp. **Japanese mayonnaise**
½ **English cucumber**
2 **avocados**
½ **lemon** for avocado
8 sheets **nori**
¼ cup **white sesame seeds**

Toppings
Ikura (salmon roe)
Tobiko (flying fish roe)

You will need:
Bamboo mat, covered with plastic wrap
Tezu (vinegared hand-dipping water): ¼ cup water + 2 tsp. rice vinegar

Note:
1. Cover the sushi rice and the completed rolls with a damp cloth at all times to prevent drying.

STEPS

1. Prepare ingredients. • Crab meat: Combine the crab meat with Japanese mayonnaise and mix together. • Cucumber: Peel and remove seeds. Cut into thin long strips, same length as the nori sheet. • Avocado: Peel, pit, and cut into ¼" (0.5 cm) thick slices. Squeeze the lemon juice over the avocado to prevent browning. • Nori sheet: Cut off ⅓ and use ⅔ sheet of nori.

2. Lay a nori sheet, shiny side down, on the bamboo mat.

3. Wet your fingers in tezu and spread 1 cup of the rice evenly onto nori sheet.

4. Sprinkle the rice with sesame seeds and turn the nori sheet over so that the rice is facing down. Line the edge of nori sheet at the bottom of the bamboo mat.

5. Place the cucumber, crab meat, and avocado at the bottom of the nori sheet.

6. Grab the bottom edge of the mat while keeping the fillings in place with your fingers, roll it into a tight cylinder, tucking the fillings in firmly.

7. Lift the edge of the bamboo mat slightly and roll it forward while keeping gentle pressure on the mat.

8. With a very sharp knife, cut each roll in half and then cut each half into 3 pieces. Remember to clean the knife with a damp cloth after every few cuts.

GLUTEN FREE
DAIRY FREE

GYUDON

• • •

 SERVES: 2

 PREP: 5 MIN

 COOK: 15 MIN

When I need to prepare a quick meal, gyudon is always at the top of my list. This tender beef with flavorful onion sauce over rice is also one of my favorite comfort foods.

INGREDIENTS

1 Tbsp. **oil**

1 large **onion,** sliced

¾ lb. (12 oz, 340 g) **thinly sliced beef,** cut into 2 inch width

2 tsp. **sugar**

2 Tbsp. **sake**

2 Tbsp. **mirin**

1 Tbsp. **soy sauce** (use tamari if gluten-free)

3 large **eggs,** beaten

2 **green onions/scallions,** finely sliced

3 cups **cooked Japanese rice**

Pickled red ginger for garnish

STEPS

1. Heat the oil in a large frying pan over medium high heat and cook the onions until softened.

2. Add the meat and sugar and cook until browned.

3. Add sake, mirin, and soy sauce and reduce the heat; simmer until most of the liquid is gone.

4. Slowly and evenly drizzle the beaten egg over the beef. Cook covered until the egg is done.

5. Add the green onion right before removing from the heat.

6. Place the beef and egg on top of steamed rice and pour desired amount of sauce. Top with pickled red ginger.

GLUTEN FREE

DAIRY FREE

KITSUNE UDON

• • •

 SERVES: 2

 PREP: 5 MIN

COOK: 10 MIN

Did you know Kitsune Udon literary means "Fox Udon"? The name refers to the light brown color of the deep fried tofu (inari age/abura age) on the udon.

INGREDIENTS

4 cups **dashi**
2 servings of **udon**
2 **inariage** (seasoned fried tofu pouch), cut in half
1 **green onion/scallion**, finely sliced

Seasonings
2 Tbsp. **soy sauce** (use tamari if gluten-free)
2 Tbsp. **mirin**
2 tsp. **sugar**
¼ tsp. **salt**

Toppings (optional)
Blanched spinach, cut into 2" (5 cm) pieces
Narutomaki (fish cake), thinly sliced

STEPS

1. In a medium saucepan, add dashi and the seasonings and bring to a boil. Add the udon and cook for 3-5 minutes.

2. Serve udon and soup in bowls and top with inariage, spinach, narutomaki, and green onion.

Notes:
1. You can use any kind of udon, but I like frozen sanuki udon from Asian supermarkets. If you use frozen udon, you don't have to defrost prior to cooking.

GLUTEN FREE
DAIRY FREE

OMURICE

• • •

 SERVES: 2 - 3

 PREP: 5 MIN

COOK: 20 MIN

In Japan, many restaurants that serve western food offer omurice on their menu. It's a sweet tomato-flavored chicken fried rice wrapped in a soft egg shell. I love extra ketchup on mine.

INGREDIENTS

For Chicken Fried Rice

1 Tbsp. **olive oil**

½ medium **onion**, finely chopped

1 **chicken thigh**, rinsed and pat dry, cut into ½" (1 cm) pieces

½ cup **frozen mixed vegetables**, defrosted

Salt

Freshly ground **black pepper**

1½ cups **cooked Japanese rice**

1 Tbsp. **ketchup**

1 tsp. **soy sauce** (use tamari if gluten-free)

For 1 omelette

1 large **egg**

1 Tbsp. **milk**

1 Tbsp. **olive oil**

3 Tbsp. **sharp cheddar cheese**

STEPS

1. To make fried rice, heat the oil in a medium non-stick pan and sauté the onion until softened. Add the chicken and cook until no longer pink and add the mixed vegetables. Season with salt and pepper.

2. Add the rice, ketchup and soy sauce and combine everything evenly with a spatula. Transfer the fried rice to a plate and wash the pan.

3. To make an omelette, whisk the egg and milk together in a small bowl. Heat the oil in the pan over medium high heat. When the pan is hot, pour the egg mixture into the pan and tilt to cover the bottom of the pan. Lower the heat when the bottom of the egg has set (but still soft on top).

4. To make omurice, put the cheese and the fried rice on top of the omelette. Use the spatula to fold both sides of omelette toward the middle to cover the fried rice. Slowly move the omurice to the edge of the pan.

5. Hold a plate in one hand and the pan in the other hand, flip the pan and move the omurice to the plate. While it's still hot, cover the omurice with a paper towel and shape it into American/Rugby football shape.

6. Drizzle the ketchup on top for decoration.

GLUTEN FREE

VEGETARIAN

OYAKODON

• • •

 SERVES: 2

 PREP: 5 MIN

COOK: 15 MIN

Oyakodon translates to "parent and child" donburi, referring to the chicken and the egg used for this comforting dish.

INGREDIENTS

3 Tbsp. **mirin**

1 Tbsp. **sake**

1 cup **dashi**

2 Tbsp. **soy sauce** (use tamari if gluten-free)

1 Tbsp. **sugar**

½ large **onion,** thinly sliced

2 **chicken thighs,** rinsed and pat dry, cut into 1" (2.5 cm) pieces

2 large **eggs,** beaten

1 **mitsuba** (Japanese wild parsley) or **green onion/scallion,** chopped for garnish

3 cups **cooked Japanese rice**

STEPS

1. Add mirin and sake in a large frying pan and bring to a boil over medium high heat. Add dashi, soy sauce, and sugar and bring to a boil again.

2. Add the onion in a single layer and place the chicken on top. Cover and bring to a boil.

3. Skim off the scum and fat and cook over medium heat for about 10 minutes.

4. Slowly and evenly drizzle the beaten egg over the chicken and onion. Cook covered until the egg is done.

5. Add the mitsuba right before removing from the heat.

6. Put the chicken and egg on top of steamed rice and pour desired amount of sauce.

GLUTEN FREE

DAIRY FREE

JUSTONECOOKBOOK.COM

SOBA SALAD

• • •

A party favorite, this sweet, spicy, and tangy soba salad is very easy to put together. Light and refreshing, it's perfect for hot summer days!

SERVES: 4

PREP: 10 MIN

COOK: 5 MIN

INGREDIENTS

9 oz (3 bundles) **soba/buckwheat noodles** (use wheat-free soba noodles if gluten-free)

½ cup chopped **green onion/scallion**

¼ cup chopped **cilantro**

3 Tbsp. **sesame seeds**

For dressing

1 Tbsp. **canola** or **grapeseed oil**

3 Tbsp. **sesame oil**

½ tsp. **crushed red peppers**

3 Tbsp. **honey**

3 Tbsp. **soy sauce** (use tamari if gluten-free)

Note: You do not need to salt the water for cooking soba.

STEPS

1. To make the dressing, combine canola/grapeseed oil, sesame oil and crushed red peppers in a small microwave safe bowl and microwave on high for 3 minutes. Set aside to let it cool a bit; be careful while handling as it'll get very hot. Combine honey and soy sauce in another small bowl and add the oil mixture. Whisk all together until the honey is completely dissolved.

2. Bring water to a boil and cook the soba noodles according to the package instructions, but keep it al dente. Drain into a colander and rinse the soba under cold running water. Drain well and transfer to a large bowl.

3. Combine the soba, dressing, green onion, cilantro and sesame seeds, and toss everything together. Transfer to a serving bowl or plate. Serve chilled or at room temperature.

GLUTEN FREE

DAIRY FREE

VEGETARIAN/VEGAN

SPICY TUNA ROLL

•••

Craving some sushi rolls? With a bit of spicy sriracha, some mayo, and sashimi-grade tuna, you can enjoy this easy roll at home.

 YIELDS: 2 ROLLS

 PREP: 25 MIN

COOK: 0 MIN

INGREDIENTS

1½ cups **prepared sushi rice**

4 oz (113 g) **sashimi-grade tuna**, cut into ¼" (0.5 cm) cubes or minced

3 tsp. **Sriracha sauce**

2 tsp. chopped **green onion/scallion**

½ tsp. **sesame oil**

1 sheet **nori**, cut in half crosswise

2 Tbsp. **white roasted sesame seeds**

Spicy Mayo

1 Tbsp. **Japanese mayonnaise**

1 tsp. **Sriracha sauce**

You will need:

Bamboo mat, covered with plastic wrap

Tezu (vinegared hand-dipping water): ¼ cup water + 2 tsp. rice vinegar

Note: Cover the sushi rice and the completed rolls with a damp cloth at all times to prevent drying.

STEPS

1. Combine the tuna, Sriracha sauce, 1 tsp. green onion, and sesame oil in a medium bowl.

2. Lay a sheet of nori, shiny side down, on the bamboo mat.

3. Wet your fingers in tezu and spread ¾ cup of the rice evenly onto nori sheet.

4. Sprinkle the rice with sesame seeds and turn the sheet of nori over so that the rice side is facing down. Line the edge of nori sheet at the bottom end of the bamboo mat.

5. Place half of the tuna mixture at the bottom end of the nori sheet.

6. Grab the bottom edge of the bamboo mat while keeping the fillings in place with your fingers, roll into a tight cylinder. Lift the edge of the bamboo mat and continue to roll it forward while keeping gentle pressure on the mat.

7. With a very sharp knife, cut the roll in half and then cut each half into 3 pieces. Clean the knife with a damp cloth every few cuts.

8. To make spicy mayo, combine mayo and Sriracha sauce in a bowl and mix well. Put a dollop of spicy mayo on top of each sushi and garnish with the remaining green onion.

GLUTEN FREE

DAIRY FREE

DESSERTS

DORAYAKI......81
FLAN......83
GREEN TEA ICE CREAM......85
GREEN TEA STEAMED CAKE......87
JAPANESE CHEESECAKE......89

DORAYAKI

• • •

YIELDS: 8 PIECES

PREP: 20 MIN

COOK: 40 MIN

Dorayaki (*Japanese red bean pancake*) is a traditional Japanese confection made of two small sweet pancakes wrapped around a sweet red bean paste filling. It's light and fluffy, not overly sweet. Enjoy it with sips of green tea.

INGREDIENTS

4 large **eggs**

140 g (⅔ cup) **sugar**

2 Tbsp. **honey**

160 g (1 cup + 2 Tbsp.) **all-purpose flour**, sifted

1 tsp. **baking powder**, sifted

1-2 Tbsp. **water**

2 Tbsp. **oil**

1 can **Ogura-An** (or 18 oz/520g sweetened red bean paste)

Notes

1. Homemade sweet red bean paste recipe.

2. If you don't eat it on the same or next day (keep it in a cool place), wrap the dorayaki in plastic wrap and put in a Ziploc freezer bag to store in the freezer for up to a month.

STEPS

1. Combine eggs, sugar, and honey in a large bowl and whisk well until the mixture becomes fluffy. Add flour and baking powder into the bowl and mix all together. Keep in the fridge to rest for 15 minutes.

2. Stir in ½ Tbsp of water at a time to get the right consistency. It should be a little bit thicker than pancake batter. If the batter is too thin, pancakes will be too flat and not fluffy.

3. Heat a large non-stick frying pan over medium-low heat. Dip a paper towel in oil and coat the bottom of the pan with the oil. The pan should be slightly oiled but the oil shouldn't be visible. That's the secret to get nice texture for dorayaki.

4. With a ladle, drop the batter from 6" (15 cm) above the pan to create 3" (8 cm) diameter pancakes. When you see the surface of the batter starting to bubble, flip over and cook the other side. Transfer to a plate and cover with a damp towel to prevent drying. Continue making pancakes.

5. Make sandwich with red bean paste. Put more red bean paste in the center so the shape of dorayaki will be curved (middle part should be thicker). Wrap dorayaki with plastic wrap until ready to serve.

DAIRY FREE DF

FLAN

•••

In Japan we call this dessert "Purin" and it's very popular with both children and adults. Melt-in-your mouth custard topped with slightly bitter caramel, simply heaven.

 SERVES: 8

 PREP: 25 MIN

COOK: 15 MIN

INGREDIENTS

For Caramel Sauce
140 g (⅔ cup) **granulated sugar**
¼ cup **water**
½ cup **boiling water**

For Custard
10 g (3 tsp.) **gelatin**
¼ cup **water**
1¾ cups (400 ml) **milk**
4 large **egg yolks**
80 g (⅓ cup + 1 Tbsp.) **granulated sugar**
½ cup **heavy whipping cream**
2 tsp. **vanilla**

STEPS

1. To make caramel sauce, cook sugar and water over medium heat in a small saucepan. Gently tilt the pan off the heat to distribute color evenly as the sugar caramelizes. When the mixture turns into a nice amber color, immediately remove from heat and pour in ½ cup of boiling water and set aside.

2. Soak the ramekins under warm water for 5 seconds to heat up. This will prevent the caramel sauce from solidifying. Evenly distribute the caramel sauce in each ramekin and set aside.

3. To make custard, combine gelatin and water in a small bowl and set aside. In a small saucepan, heat half of the milk (200 ml) over medium heat until the milk is warm to the touch.

4. In a large bowl, whisk egg yolks and sugar until creamy. Temper the egg mixture with the warm milk (add slowly) while whisking. Pour the mixture back into the saucepan and cook over low heat, stirring constantly, until the mixture coats a spoon with a thin film, bubbles at the edges, or reaches 160°F (71°C).

5. Add in the gelatin mixture and mix well. Remove from the heat.

6. Pour the mixture through a fine sieve into a clean bowl sitting in an ice bath. Add the rest of the milk, heavy whipping cream and vanilla and whisk all together.

7. Pour the custard into the ramekins, and chill in the fridge for at least 1 hour.

8. To serve, run a small sharp knife around the flan to loosen. Turn over onto a plate. Shake gently to release flan.

GLUTEN FREE (GF)

GREEN TEA ICE CREAM

• • •

 YIELDS: ½ QUART

 PREP: 25 MIN

COOK: 5 MIN

This unique ice cream is made with matcha (green tea powder) giving it a bright green color. Matcha's natural bitter and rich flavor goes really well with slightly sweet cream.

INGREDIENTS

1 cup **whole milk**
1 cup **heavy whipping cream**
3 Tbsp. **green tea powder** (matcha)
½ cup **sugar**
Pinch of **salt**

STEPS

1. In a medium saucepan, whisk together whole milk, heavy whipping cream, green tea powder, sugar, and salt. Heat over medium heat, stirring often, until it starts to foam and is very hot to the touch but not boiling.

2. Remove from the heat and soak the bottom of the saucepan in ice water and cool the mixture. Cover and chill in the refrigerator for 2-3 hours.

3. Once the mixture is thoroughly chilled, transfer to a pre-chilled ice cream maker and churn according to the manufacturer's instructions (20-25 minutes).

4. Transfer the soft ice cream into an airtight container and freeze for at least 3 hours before serving.

GLUTEN FREE (GF)

GREEN TEA STEAMED CAKE

• • •

 YIELDS: 4 PIECES

 PREP: 10 MIN

COOK: 15 MIN

This delicate dessert is infused with the flavor of matcha (green tea powder) and made with egg, yogurt, honey, and a tiny bit of cooking oil. They are light, soft and moist and one of my favorite snacks.

INGREDIENTS

1 large **egg**

1 Tbsp. **canola oil**

1 Tbsp. **honey**

3 Tbsp. plain regular **yogurt**

1 ½ Tbsp. **sugar**

½ cup **all-purpose flour**, sifted

1 tsp. **baking powder**, sifted

1 tsp. **green tea powder** (matcha)

Sweet red bean paste (optional)

STEPS

1. Wrap a frying pan lid with a kitchen towel. This will prevent condensation from falling onto the cakes while steaming.

2. Place four empty ramekins in the pan and pour water into the frying pan to halfway up the exterior of the ramekins. Take out the ramekins and place a cupcake liner inside. Cover the pan with the lid, and bring water to a boil.

3. In a medium bowl, add the egg and oil and whisk well. Then add the honey, yogurt and sugar and mix until well combined.

4. Add the flour, baking powder and green tea powder. With a rubber spatula, fold in until well combined.

5. Pour the batter evenly into four cupcake liners.

6. When the water starts to boil, place the ramekins inside the pan.

7. Cover with the lid and steam over medium-low heat for 12-14 minutes, or until a wooden skewer inserted in the center of the cake comes out clean without wet batter. Do not overcook as the cakes will become hard.

8. Remove the ramekins from the pan and serve with sweet red bean paste.

JUSTONECOOKBOOK.COM

JAPANESE CHEESECAKE

• • •

 YIELD: 9-INCH CAKE

 PREP: 30 MIN

 COOK: 90 MIN

Do you like soft creamy desserts? This delicious cheesecake simply melts in your mouth. Different from New York cheesecakes, Japanese cheesecakes are very light and fluffy.

INGREDIENTS

400 g (14.1 oz) **cream cheese,** at room temperature
60 g (6 Tbsp.) **granulated sugar**
60 g (4 Tbsp.) **unsalted butter,** cut into ½" (1 cm) slices, at room temperature
6 large **egg yolks,** beaten, at room temperature
200 ml **heavy whipping cream,** at room temperature
10 ml (2 tsp.) **lemon juice**
1 Tbsp. **rum** (optional)
80 g (8 Tbsp.) **all-purpose flour,** sifted twice
3 Tbsp. **apricot jam**
1 tsp. **water**

For Meringue
6 large **egg whites,** refrigerated
100g (10 Tbsp.) **granulated sugar** for meringue

STEPS

1. Lightly grease the bottom and sides of a 9" (23 cm) spring-form pan with cooking spray and line with parchment paper. Wrap the base of the cake pan with aluminium foil (preferably with extra-large heavy duty foil) to prevent seepage.

2. Preheat oven to 320°F (160°C). Start boiling water.

3. In the bowl of the electric mixer, beat the cream cheese and sugar on medium-high speed until smooth. In the following order, add one ingredient at a time and mix until thoroughly incorporated: butter, beaten egg yolk, heavy cream, lemon juice, rum, and flour.

4. Transfer the batter to a large bowl. Wash the mixer bowl and dry completely. Make sure there is no oil or water in the bowl.

5. To make meringue, beat the egg whites until stiff peaks form (See Note for detailed directions). Be careful not to overbeat because the surface of the cake will crack.

Recipe continued on next page.

JAPANESE CHEESECAKE

● ● ●

Recipe continued from page 89.

STEPS

6. Add one-third of the meringue to the batter and mix well first. Then add the rest of the meringue all at once and fold it in.

7. Pour the batter in the cake pan and then drop the pan from 2-3" (5-7 cm) high to the countertop to remove any air bubbles.

8. Place the cake pan in a large roasting pan and pour 1" (2.5 cm) of boiling water in the roasting pan. Place the roasting pan in the middle rack of the oven.

9. Bake at 320°F (160°C) for 60 minutes or until light golden brown. Then reduce temperature to 300°F (150°C) and bake for another 30 minutes. When a wooden skewer inserted in the center of the cake comes out clean without wet batter, turn off the oven. Let the cake sit in the oven with the door slightly ajar for 15 minutes.

10. Remove from the oven. Take out the cake pan from the roasting pan, and let it cool on a wire rack. In a small bowl, heat apricot jam and water in microwave for 30 seconds and spread the jam on top of the cake. When the cake is completely cool, take it out from the pan and refrigerate for a few hours before serving.

Notes:

1. How To Beat Egg Whites To Stiff Peaks: Beat the egg whites until frothy on low speed. Then add one-third of the sugar and increase the speed to medium. Gradually add the sugar one-third at a time as the mixer runs. Once all of the sugar has been added, increase mixer speed to high and whip for approximately 4 minutes, until the egg whites have doubled in volume and are thick and glossy. To test, the peaks should stand straight up when you lift up the beater. If the egg whites have not reached the desired consistency, continue whipping at high speed for another 30 seconds, then stop and test again. Once the egg whites are over beaten, they can't be used for the recipe.

2. Leave the oven door ajar because sudden temperature change will result in collapse of the cake.

RECIPE INDEX

11

13

15

17

25

27

29

31

33

37

39

41

43

45

49

51

Recipe Notes

Recipe Notes

Printed in Great Britain
by Amazon